I0045215

A Guide to Healing, Hustling, and Building Wealth on Your Terms

by Trinetta M. Henderson

THE BOSS MOM EFFECT

For permissions and inquiries, contact:

H.E.R. Legacy Works

Merrillville, Indiana

thenderson2006@msn.com

ISBN: 979-8-9994428-0-2

Printed in the United States of America

Dedication

To every mother who ever wondered if she was doing enough—
This is for you.

To the women who rise before the sun,
Who give without applause,
Who carry both dreams and diapers, pain and power—
You are not invisible. You are unstoppable.

To Eric, Tristian, and Naomi—
You were my reason before I ever found my voice.
Everything I built, I built with you in mind.

And to the little girl I used to be—
You didn't just survive.
You became everything you needed.
I'm so proud of you.

This book is for every woman daring to build something beautiful out of brokenness.
May you find yourself in these pages.
May you know—without a doubt—that you are already a Boss Mom.

With love,
Trinetta M. Henderson

Foreword

If you are holding this book, I want you to know something:
You are already enough.
Even if you're tired. Even if you're behind. Even if you're holding
it all together with faith, coffee, and silent tears.

You're here. And that means you're ready.

This is not a book about perfection. This is not a book that tells
you to hustle until you burn out.
This is a book about becoming—a woman, a mother, a leader who
chooses healing, success, and financial freedom on her own terms.

My name is Trinetta M. Henderson, and I was born and raised on
the South Side of Chicago in the lively heart of Hyde Park. I
became a mom at 17, joined the Army at 18, and spent years
pushing through survival mode to figure out how to thrive—for
myself and for my children.

There were times I felt invisible. There were moments I felt
ashamed. There were days I wanted to give up.
But deep down, I knew I was meant for more.
And that "more" wasn't just for me—it was for my children, my
lineage, and every mother like me who just needed someone to
show her the way.

That's why I wrote The Boss Mom Effect.

This book is part memoir, part blueprint, and part love letter to the
women who are doing the impossible every single day.
Women who don't have a safety net. Women who are building
while healing.
Women who are brave enough to break generational cycles and

still make breakfast before the sun comes up.

You'll read about my mistakes, my breakthroughs, my systems, my faith, and my freedom.
You'll meet the woman I used to be—and the woman I fought to become.
And by the end, I hope you'll meet yourself in a new, more powerful way.

This book is not just for single moms.
It's for every mother.
Every grandmother.
Every foster mom.
Every woman raising a child and building a dream at the same time.

Because when one of us rises, we all rise.
That's the Boss Mom Effect.

So take a deep breath.
Know that you are seen.
Know that you are not alone.
Know that everything you desire is still possible—even now.

Let's begin.

— Trinetta M. Henderson

Chapter 1: The Call to Rise

There comes a moment in every woman's life when silence becomes unbearable—not because it is loud, but because of what it reveals. That moment for me came after years of hustling, pushing, striving, and sacrificing—when I finally paused and had to face myself. Not the version of me I presented to the world, but the me that was worn down beneath layers of responsibility and survival.

I was a mother before I became a woman in full bloom. I had three children by the time I was 21, and while other girls my age were finding themselves, traveling the world, and discovering their spiritual identities- I was learning budget, potty training, and feeding three mouths before I fed my own. Let me be clear, my children were never a burden. But the expectations placed on me, the lack of support, and the unspoken rule that I had to hold it all together with a smile- that was the burden.

Being a mother so young made me grow up faster, but it also caused me to bury parts of myself prematurely. I tucked away dreams I couldn't afford to chase. I suppressed tears I didn't have time to cry. I learned how to survive without ever being taught how to thrive.

Answering the call to rise wasn't a moment—it was a slow awakening. A crawl back to my divine self. But that awakening didn't come through spa days or dream boards. It came through hard nights and soul-stretching choices. It came through the military.

Yes, I served. I served with pride, discipline, and fierce devotion. Being in the Army taught me how to push past my limits, how to show up even when I didn't feel like it, and how to lead with both my mind and my presence. It gave me courage, discipline, leadership skills, and a financial head start. It was a way out and a chance to begin rewriting my story, but it came at cost to my softness. I remember standing in formation, boots planted, eyes forward, wondering if anyone could see how exhausted I really was. Not just physically—but emotionally. I gave to my country, my children, my job, my community. But who poured back into me?

The military shaped me. But it didn't heal me. That part would come later- when I decided to become my own safe place. It wasn't easy. Healing never is. I had to confront truths I had long buried. I had to grieve the girl who had to grow up too soon. I had to forgive myself for the years I was just surviving. I had to look in the mirror and admit that I was tired of being strong for everyone else. I wanted to be soft- for me.

This book was born from that moment—when I slowly began to change.

I realized that just working wasn't going to get me to where I wanted to be, I needed to build a business. Not just to escape the 9-5, but to have a legacy. I understood the importance of proving to my children that you can lead, heal, and thrive at the same time. That softness is not weakness. That rest is not laziness. That Black women deserve joy- not just resilience.

There is one night that still lingers with me. The kids were asleep. I was sitting on my bed, the light of my laptop flickering against my face, scrolling through business ideas, tears quietly slipping down my cheeks. Not because I was sad- but because I realized I was still dreaming. After all these years, I still had dreams. And that meant hope was still alive in me.

I started journaling again. Not just about business goals, but about the woman I wanted to become. I wrote letters to my future self. I wrote prayers not just to make it from day to day, but for abundance, softness, and freedom. I started listening to "The Habits of A Goddess" podcast. I even began creating my own affirmations and taping them to my vanity mirror. I spoke life over myself, even when I didn't believe the words yet.

Every decision to rise became sacred. Cooking a healthy meal. Listening to sermons by Joel Osteen and TD Jakes while walking the dog. Asking for help. Charging what I was worth. Blocking toxic energy. All of it mattered.

And here's what I learned: rising isn't about perfection. It's about alignment. It's about choosing yourself every day- even when it's inconvenient. It's about learning to hear your own voice above the noise of the world. My call to rise wasn't a single moment. It was a thousand decisions over time. And each one, no matter how small, brought me closer to the woman I was always meant to be.

Your call to rise may not look like mine. It might not involve motherhood, the military, or entrepreneurship. It may be a call to finally rest. To go back to school and get that degree. To leave a relationship. To write the book or to heal trauma. Whatever your rise looks like, know this: it is valid. It is sacred. It is necessary.

The world doesn't benefit from your burnout. It benefits from your brilliance.

You do not owe anyone an explanation for why you want more. Wanting more is not selfish, it's life sustaining. Especially when you know the cost of settling.

I'm not writing this from a place of having arrived. I'm writing this in the trenches of transformation. But I have seen what is possible. I've tasted what it feels like to live in alignment. I've cried tears of joy from simply feeling safe in my own skin.

This is your invitation. Not to hustle more- but to honor more. To honor the quiet whispers of your spirit. To honor your softness, your needs, your voice.

So I ask you: what are you waiting for? Your life is not on pause. Your purpose is not postponed. You don't need anyone's approval. You are the sign you have been waiting for. And the moment you decide to rise, everything else around you will have no choice but to follow suit. Not instantly- but inevitably.

Reflection:
What parts of you have been silenced in the name of survival? Where have you ignored your own voice to meet the demands of others? What would it look like to finally answer the call within you? Who might you become if you believed you were already worthy?

Affirmation:
I am no longer waiting for permission to be powerful. I rise boldly, consistently, and unapologetically. My past shaped me, but it does not limit me. I am the legacy my ancestors prayed for. I give myself permission to thrive.

Prayer: For the Strength to Rise
Divine Creator,

Thank You for the strength within me that never died, only waited. Thank You for the whispers that call me back to my true self. Remind me daily that I am not behind. I am being built. Give me the courage to rise—even when no one claps, even when fear is loud. Help me to lead with softness, stand with purpose, and build with vision. Heal the parts of me that are still afraid to be seen. I am ready. Amen.

Chapter 2: Healing the Wounds Hustle Hid

"My rest is righteous. My softness is sacred."

I was so busy hustling that I didn't realize I was hurting.

Hustle had become my badge of honor—and my bandage. It allowed me to show the world I was capable, resilient, unstoppable. But beneath that constant motion was a woman unraveling. Not visibly. Not loudly. Just quietly falling apart inside the rhythm of responsibilities that never paused. I didn't see it as a wound because it looked like success. But success that costs you yourself is not success. It's self-neglect wrapped in productivity.

There's a particular type of pain that comes with being strong for too long. And for Black women, that strength is often inherited—passed down from grandmothers who endured, mothers who survived, and communities that praised us not for resting, but for doing more with less. Rest wasn't part of the equation. Neither was softness. You had to be tough, had to keep going, had to keep proving yourself. To stop was to fail. Or at least, that's what we were taught.

I didn't know I needed healing because I had never been taught to stop. The grind was my gospel. I wore my exhaustion like a trophy. If I could just outwork my pain, maybe I could outrun it.

From the moment I became a mother at 17, I believed slowing down wasn't an option. My babies needed diapers, food, stability. I didn't have a village. I *was* the village. I had to show up, keep going, get the degree, hold down the job, smile through the stress. Every win was celebrated—but no one ever asked what it cost me. Not even me.

Eventually, I stopped asking myself too.

The Hustle Wasn't Just a Grind. It Was a Shield.

I wore ambition like armor. I sharpened my schedule like a sword. I learned how to suppress tears in public, how to pour from an empty cup, how to grind past grief. I became so good at appearing okay that even I forgot what not being okay felt like. In doing so, I became a master of surviving—but I lost sight of what *thriving* could feel like.

There's a moment I'll never forget. I was standing in my kitchen, staring blankly into the fridge—not because I was hungry, but because I couldn't remember what I was looking for. My mind was fogged. My body was tense. My spirit was disconnected. I had just come home from work, the kids were arguing in the background, the laundry buzzer was going off, and all I could think was: *Is this it?*

That night, I cried in the shower for 45 minutes. Not because of one big thing—but because of *every little thing* I had been carrying silently. That was my soul's whisper becoming a scream. That was the moment I knew something had to change.

Healing didn't come easy. It didn't arrive wrapped in comfort or clarity. It felt foreign. It felt indulgent. And at times, it felt like failure. I had to unlearn the belief that my value was tied to my productivity. That was a deep wound, and wounds don't heal overnight.

Learning to Sit With Myself Was the First Step

At first, healing looked like doing less—and that terrified me. I remember sitting on the couch one day, exhausted from work, and instead of folding laundry or answering emails, I just… sat. No TV. No scrolling. No pretending to be okay. Just silence.

And in that silence, memories surfaced. Wounds I had buried beneath busyness began to breathe again. The kind of memories you avoid because they don't fit neatly into your narrative of being "strong."

I was forced to confront the abandonment I felt from my father. The shame I carried as a young single mom who had to grow up while still feeling like a child. The pain of friendships that only existed when I was useful. The exhaustion of always being "the strong one" — the one who doesn't get checked on, only leaned on.

So I wrote. I prayed. I cried. I sat with the discomfort instead of running from it.

I forgave the girl who got pregnant before she was ready. I forgave the woman who stayed in jobs and relationships that dimmed her light because she believed survival was the only option. I even forgave the parts of me that had judged my own softness as weakness.

Healing Taught Me How to Feel Again

I had gone numb from years of pushing through. I didn't even realize it until joy started to feel unfamiliar. I could smile, laugh, post the right photos — but when I was alone, I felt... nothing. Like a well that had run dry but was still being pumped for water.

So when I began healing, I didn't just cry — I *felt*. And that was more radical than any hustle I had ever done. I felt grief for the years I couldn't get back. I felt compassion for the young woman I was — doing her best with what she had. I felt anger toward the systems and cycles that taught me I had to be everything for everyone. And then, slowly… I felt relief.

I learned how to rest. Not just physically, but spiritually. Rest became my rebellion. I stopped equating rest with laziness. I stopped needing to "earn" my peace. I made room for slow mornings, long prayers, deep breaths, and empty space.

I learned how to receive. Compliments. Help. Stillness. Grace. All things I had once rejected in the name of "I got it." Because the truth was—I didn't. And I wasn't supposed to. Healing helped me understand that interdependence is not weakness. It's wisdom.

I learned that I didn't have to hustle for love or labor for worthiness. I was already enough. Even when I was unproductive. Even when I was undone.

Redefining the Hustle

The hardest part wasn't the pain—it was learning to be gentle with myself in the process.

Gentleness didn't come easy. I was used to grinding. To tough love. To proving myself. But healing introduced me to a softer, slower version of power—the kind that doesn't scream, doesn't hustle, doesn't apologize for existing.

As I healed, my hustle changed too. It became more sacred. I wasn't grinding to escape poverty—I was building to create legacy. I wasn't operating from fear—I was moving from fullness. And that changed everything.

I stopped chasing clients who didn't value my time. I stopped discounting my rates to be liked. I stopped overdelivering just to feel worthy. I stopped apologizing for choosing rest over burnout.

Healing didn't mean I lost my drive. It meant I started driving from a healthier place.

Success wasn't about how much I could do—it became about how much I could *feel while doing it*. Was I aligned? Was I present? Was I building something that nourished me back?

The Shift Wasn't Instant—But It Was Permanent

I began redefining success. It wasn't just money or metrics. It was joy. Peace. Alignment. It was being able to pick my kids up from school without rushing. It was having the energy to dance in the kitchen after dinner. It was not needing a vacation to recover from my everyday life.

I started noticing what drained me—and I gave myself permission to walk away. I canceled things. I missed calls. I rescheduled meetings. Not because I was irresponsible—but because I was reclaiming my life.

I invested in therapy. I took days off without guilt. I made boundaries my new love language. I stopped trying to explain myself to people committed to misunderstanding me.

And most importantly? I started telling the truth.

Telling the Truth Set Me Free

I told the truth to myself first. I admitted where I was still hurting. I named what I was tired of carrying. I allowed myself to say, "This is too much," without guilt. That kind of honesty cracked me open—but it also stitched me back together.

Then I told the truth to my children. I stopped pretending to be perfect. I shared my past with intention, not shame. I let them see me rest, cry, breathe, set boundaries, and choose joy—not just grind. And in doing so, I gave them permission to do the same one day.

I told the truth to my clients. I stopped marketing from a place of fear and started speaking from my soul. I let them see the whole woman—not just the polished brand. I talked about boundaries. About alignment. About healing. And do you know what happened? They trusted me more. Because real always resonates.

Healing is contagious.

It liberated my voice. My vision. My value. And most importantly—it gave me back to myself.

Letting Go of the Superwoman Myth

There is no medal for martyrdom. No trophy for burnout. No crown for carrying it all alone.

I had to let go of the "superwoman" mask. I had to lay it down and decide that being well was more important than being impressive. That choosing me wasn't selfish—it was sacred.

And while the world may still praise hustle, I now honor the sacred necessity of healing. Because when a woman heals, everything she touches transforms. Her home. Her business. Her body. Her relationships. Her legacy.

This Isn't the End of the Hustle. It's the Rebirth of It.

I still hustle—but now it's holy. It's rooted in peace, not panic. Purpose, not performance. My work doesn't own me. My value doesn't depend on how full my calendar is. I create from overflow, not depletion.

I still get tired—but I rest now. I still dream big—but I chase those dreams gently. I still build—but now I build with boundaries.

Healing has become my strategy. My soft power. My non-negotiable. Because a healed woman doesn't just survive the world—she reshapes it.

Reflection

Where have you been using hustle to hide your hurt?
What does rest look like for you—not just physically, but emotionally and spiritually?
Who would you become if you truly believed your worth wasn't tied to your work?

Affirmation

I am healing, whole, and worthy—without performance.
I release the pressure to prove and embrace the grace to receive.
My rest is righteous. My softness is sacred. I give myself permission to be.

Prayer: For Healing Beyond Hustle

Dear God,
Thank You for seeing the parts of me I've hidden beneath my to-do lists.
Thank You for reminding me that healing is not weakness—it is wisdom.

Show me how to slow down without fear. Restore my joy. Revive my rest.
Teach me to trust that I don't have to earn what is already mine: peace, love, and purpose.
Amen.

Chapter 3: The Power of the Pivot

"I didn't need to burn everything down to rise. I just needed to realign."

There is a sacred moment when a woman decides she's had enough—not out of bitterness, but out of clarity. That moment is called the pivot. And for many of us, the pivot doesn't come in crisis. It comes in the quiet. In the stillness after years of grinding, performing, and holding it all together. It comes in the tension between who you've been and who you're becoming.

I didn't pivot because everything was falling apart. I pivoted because everything that used to make sense... no longer did. The job that once felt secure started to feel suffocating. The hustle that once felt validating started to feel like a trap. The applause I used to chase no longer satisfied me. I wanted peace. I wanted ownership. I wanted my life back.

I didn't want to prove I could do it all—I wanted the *freedom* to decide what was truly worth doing. The pivot wasn't impulsive. It was intentional. It was spiritual. It was soul-led.

At first, I questioned myself. I wondered if I was being ungrateful or unrealistic. I had a stable job. A roof over my head. Responsibilities. People depending on me. But deep down, I knew the truth: **stability is not the same as alignment.** I was surviving well, but I wasn't living fully. And no paycheck is worth your purpose.

The Whisper That Starts It All

The pivot begins with a whisper. A nudge in your spirit. Something that says: *This isn't all there is.* For me, it was a subtle but growing ache — the kind that says, *I'm proud of what I've built, but I know I'm meant for more.*

I stopped asking for permission. I started studying.

And that's where everything changed.

I studied the wealthy. I listened to podcasts, read books, followed financial leaders who weren't just rich—but wise. I didn't care about flashy lifestyles. I wanted *strategy*. I wanted *systems*. I wanted the mindset that built empires quietly and generationally.

Bill Gates, Jeff Bezos, and Grant Cardone became my unexpected mentors. Not because I idolized them—but because I was a student of patterns. I wanted to understand how they thought. How they made decisions. How they moved in the world with vision and clarity.

I listened to Dave Ramsey say, *"People need to stop being stupid with money."* And I'll be honest—it stung. But it was a wake-up call. I wasn't stupid, but I was **uninformed**. And that ignorance was expensive.

From Struggle to Strategy

So I got serious. I tracked every dollar. I sold gently used items on Poshmark. I drove Lyft on weekends. I cut out unnecessary subscriptions. I couponed. I negotiated bills. I humbled myself financially—but not emotionally. Because humility doesn't mean smallness. It means stewardship.

Every little shift began to add up. I used the money I saved to pay off debt, build credit, and eventually invest in myself. I bought books. Took online classes. Enrolled in courses that taught me how to turn my ideas into income.

I no longer wanted to look rich. I wanted to *be* wealthy. There's a difference.

Looking rich is performance. Being wealthy is power. And power—real power—is quiet. It's compound interest. It's generational planning. It's owning your time.

The deeper I went, the more I healed. And the more I healed, the more my finances healed too. Because money and mindset are married. They either multiply together—or they sabotage each other.

Money and Mindset Are Married

If you believe you're unworthy, you'll sabotage every blessing.
If you believe love must be earned through suffering, you'll keep choosing the hard road—even when the easy one is right in front of you.
If you believe you're meant to struggle just because your mama did, you'll resist your breakthrough.

I had to heal the part of me that thought abundance was for *other people*. The part of me that felt guilty spending money on myself. The part of me that confused hustle with value. The part that thought I had to apologize for outgrowing what no longer fit.

I claimed abundance as my birthright.

Not as a luxury. Not as a reward. But as my *birthright*. And when you claim something that deeply, you begin to move differently. You begin to budget differently. To speak differently. To dream differently. Because you're no longer trying to *deserve* it — you're preparing to *receive* it.

I stopped waiting to feel "ready." I got ready in motion. I created a vision for my life—not just a to-do list. I didn't want trinkets. I wanted **territory**. Acres of land, not a closet full of Jordans. Family wealth, not financial panic. Ownership, not obligation.

And most of all—I wanted **time freedom.**

I dreamed of a life where I woke up and *chose* how I spent my day. Not one dictated by a punch clock, a manager, or a survival budget. A life where I had the freedom to rest, create, travel, pour into my kids, and make decisions from a place of vision—not urgency.

That vision lit a fire in me.

The Rise of the Boss Mom Within

I started my own business. I didn't have a fancy website, investors, or perfect branding. I had **clarity** and **conviction.** And that was enough to start. I made mistakes. I undercharged. I worked too many hours at first. I said yes when I should've said no. But I learned. And I kept going.

I reinvested in myself before I had a crowd cheering. I raised my prices. I walked away from people-pleasing. I stopped begging for seats at tables I could build myself. I realized: **every 'no' to distraction was a 'yes' to destiny.**

That was the pivot.

The pivot isn't a destination. It's a practice.

It's not a one-time moment. It's a way of life. A choice you make every day to say, *I want better—and I'm willing to move differently to get it.*

I pivoted from scarcity to sufficiency.
From fear to faith.
From hustle to harmony.

Every time life tried to pull me back into old patterns—chasing approval, shrinking myself, putting everyone else first—I reminded myself: *I'm not that woman anymore.*

She was brave. She got me here.
But she can't take me further.
And that's okay.

Loving the Woman I Once Was—Outgrowing Her Anyway

There's a strange kind of grief that comes with outgrowing your old life. It's not loud. It's not dramatic. It's subtle. Like walking out of a room you used to live in and realizing the furniture no longer fits you.

You can love the past version of yourself and still outgrow her. You can honor her without returning to her.

I had to sit with that. Because part of me felt guilty for wanting more. For shifting. For pivoting. Especially when other people were content staying the same. But just because *they're comfortable doesn't mean you have to stay stuck.*

Your spirit knows when it's time to evolve. Your body will feel it. Your peace will demand it.

Pivoting isn't just about business—it's about **belief**.

What do you believe is possible for you?
What do you believe you deserve?
What do you believe about rest, about motherhood, about success?

Those answers don't just shape your mindset—they *shape your money, your relationships, your boundaries, and your legacy.*

I didn't need to burn everything down to rise. I just needed to realign. To shift with purpose. To move from autopilot to intention.

Legacy Over Lifestyle

I stopped romanticizing grind culture. I stopped chasing clout. I stopped trying to prove I was "worthy" of being in certain rooms.

I no longer shrink to fit budgets I've outgrown.
I no longer beg for access to places I was born to lead in.
I don't trade my peace for popularity.

My pivot taught me that I'm not just here to survive—I'm here to *build.*
And not just for me—but for every woman watching. Every daughter learning. Every future generation rising behind me.

Because when a woman pivots with purpose, it opens the path for others to do the same. It says: *You can change your mind. You can evolve. You can start over—softly, powerfully, completely.*

You don't have to have it all figured out to pivot.
You just need to be honest about what's no longer working—and courageous enough to believe that something better is possible.

Reflection

What areas of your life are calling for a pivot?
Where have you been settling for survival instead of building for legacy?
What mindset shift would change everything for you right now?

Affirmation

I release the need to look wealthy and claim my right to be wealthy.
I trust my pivot. I honor my evolution.
I build not for attention—but for legacy.

Prayer: For Courage to Pivot

God of new beginnings,
Thank You for reminding me that change is not failure—it is faith.
Give me the courage to pivot, the clarity to discern what no longer serves me,
And the wisdom to build what aligns with my calling.
Help me to move with grace, grow with purpose, and release the fear that keeps me small.
I trust where You're taking me.
Amen.

Chapter 4: When the Dream Feels Too Big

"The dream isn't too big — your faith is still stretching to hold it."

There comes a point in every purpose-driven woman's life when the very dream she prayed for starts to feel like a burden. Not because it isn't beautiful, but because it's bigger than she imagined. Heavier. Louder. More sacred. That's when fear tries to creep in — not the kind that screams, but the kind that whispers:

"Who do you think you are to dream that big?"

And the truth is… I almost believed it.

There's something terrifying about being entrusted with a vision that feels larger than your current life. It confronts every self-doubt you've ever buried. It shows you the gaps between who you've been and who you're becoming. And if you're not careful, you'll start shrinking the dream to fit your fear — instead of stretching your faith to fit the dream.

I remember when the vision for my business and legacy first arrived. It didn't tiptoe into my life. It crashed through like a tidal wave — sudden, divine, and undeniable. One minute I was brainstorming ways to make a little extra money, and the next I was planning how to buy real estate, launch a coaching platform, publish a book, and build something my great-grandchildren could inherit.

It wasn't just a business idea. It was a calling. And it scared me more than anything I'd ever said yes to.

Big Dreams Expose Small Beliefs

It's easy to dream small. Safe dreams don't require faith — they just require familiarity. But a *God-sized dream* will drag every insecurity into the light. It will stretch your confidence. It will pull on the places you've healed and the ones you haven't.

Suddenly you're not just thinking about branding or pricing — you're confronting the little girl in you who was told she wasn't smart enough. The woman in you who wonders if she's too old. The mom in you who feels guilty chasing a dream when the kids still need dinner and help with homework.

Big dreams will find every reason you think you're unqualified and hold them up like a mirror. But here's what I've learned:

God doesn't give dreams based on your résumé. God gives dreams based on your readiness to surrender.

You don't have to be the most educated. You don't have to have the biggest following. You just have to be *available* — willing to say yes before the how fully shows up. The size of the dream isn't the problem. It's the size of your **trust** trying to catch up.

From Fear to Fire

At first, I tried to shrink the dream. I told myself I'd start small—test the waters, take the "reasonable" route. I wanted to protect myself from disappointment. I thought I was being practical, wise, mature. But let's be honest: I was afraid.

And fear doesn't always yell. Sometimes it disguises itself as logic.
"Let's be realistic."
"Maybe next year."
"What if it doesn't work?"

But every time I tried to play it safe, the vision burned in my chest like an untamed fire. It refused to be boxed in. It refused to be postponed. It refused to be treated like a hobby when it was divinely designed to be my harvest.

So I had to choose: obey the fear or trust the fire.

I trusted the fire.

That trust didn't mean I suddenly had a business plan, a full team, or funding. It meant I was *willing* to move forward with obedience even when clarity hadn't fully caught up. I had to learn that *obedience opens doors that overthinking never will.*

There were days I felt overwhelmed. Days I cried. Days I looked at other women succeeding and felt like I was stuck in the waiting room of my own dream. But I stayed anchored in one truth:

If God gave me the dream, then She already prepared the way.

My job wasn't to master the blueprint. My job was to say yes to the assignment.

Saying Yes Before It Makes Sense

Saying yes looked like investing in my growth when my bank account didn't match my vision.
Saying yes looked like creating late at night after my kids went to bed.
Saying yes looked like turning down good opportunities that weren't *God* opportunities.

It meant protecting my peace from conversations that doubted my capacity. It meant surrounding myself with women who wouldn't flinch when I spoke million-dollar dreams out loud. It meant canceling self-doubt on a daily basis and deciding to believe *again and again* that I was chosen for this.

I didn't need to be ready. I just needed to be *available.*

Each time I moved forward, even in fear, I saw confirmation. Resources showed up. Clients found me. Creative downloads poured in. Doors opened that I hadn't even knocked on.

Not because I was perfect. Not because I had it all figured out. But because I was *in position.*

When the Dream Feels Heavy, Remember This

When the dream feels too big, it's because it isn't meant to be done in your strength alone. That's the whole point. If you could do it without divine help, it wouldn't be a calling — it would just be a project.

There were moments I sat in front of my vision board with tears in my eyes. Not because I didn't believe — but because belief requires *energy*. And I was tired. I was mothering, working, building, and barely holding it together. I kept asking, *"God, why would You give me something this big when You know how tired I am?"*

And the answer I heard in my spirit was clear:
"Because I trust you to carry it the right way — with Me."

God-sized dreams require God-sized dependence. They're not designed to crush you. They're designed to **form** you.

They teach you to:

- Listen more closely
- Walk more humbly
- Rest more deeply
- Surrender more often

They make you confront your impatience, your perfectionism, and your pride. They show you the places where you've been operating in hustle, not holiness.

The dream isn't here to break you. It's here to **build you.**

Your Dream Is Not Too Big—Your Environment Was Just Too Small

I used to think I needed to get smaller to be more successful. I thought if I was more polite, more humble, more "relatable," more quiet about my desires — maybe the world would accept me.

But the truth is, *the wrong room will always feel too tight for a woman who's outgrown her limitations.*

Once I started placing my vision in the right environments — around other women who weren't afraid of abundance — everything changed.

I stopped shrinking.
I stopped doubting.
I stopped apologizing for wanting what I wanted.

In those rooms, no one flinched when I said I wanted land, luxury, legacy, and peace. They *nodded.* They *affirmed.* They held space for the fullness of me — and I did the same for them.

You Are the Answer to a Generational Prayer

There is a kind of dream that doesn't just come to you — it *moves through* you. A dream that carries the weight of your bloodline. A

31

dream your ancestors whispered about. A dream born from women who couldn't afford to chase theirs... so they passed the baton to you.

That's what this is.

You are the continuation of their courage.

Your dream isn't just about building a business or buying land or publishing a book. It's about breaking cycles. Shifting lineage. Rewriting the family narrative. Turning struggle into strategy and pain into purpose.

And that kind of dream will feel heavy sometimes. But it is holy.

When the dream feels too big, remember: *it didn't choose you because you were perfect. It chose you because you're faithful.*

You are the kind of woman who rises, even when her legs are trembling. You are the kind of woman who builds, even while healing. You are the kind of woman who says *yes*, even when she doesn't see the full map.

And that is why the dream chose you.

You Don't Need More Time. You Need More Trust.

Your dream is waiting on your belief, not your perfection. Every delay, every detour, every "not yet" wasn't denial — it was preparation.

You're not behind. You're being built.

You don't need to hustle harder. You need to soften your heart toward what's already yours. Let go of the timeline. Let go of the need to control every outcome. Let go of comparing your path to anyone else's.

Your dream is safe in your hands because your heart is aligned with something eternal.

And the moment you stop trying to carry it alone, you'll feel the divine support rushing in.

So here's what I say to the woman who's standing at the edge of her next big leap:
You are not too late.
You are not too broken.
You are not too much.

You are *becoming*.

Reflection

- What have you believed disqualifies you from your biggest dreams?
- Who or what have you allowed to shrink your vision?
- What would it look like to believe that the dream *chose* you — and not the other way around?

Affirmation

My dream is not too big—my faith is expanding to match it.
I trust the vision. I trust the process. I trust the God who gave it to me.
I do not shrink. I rise.

Prayer: For Strength When the Vision Feels Heavy

God of every dream You've ever whispered into my spirit—
Thank You for trusting me with this vision. Thank You for not
letting me settle.
Thank You for stretching me even when I wanted to stay safe.
When the dream feels too heavy, remind me that I was never
meant to carry it alone.
Teach me to partner with You. To plan boldly. To move in faith.
And to build with joy.
I am ready. I believe. I receive.
Amen.

Chapter 5: The Cost of Becoming Her

"Becoming her will cost you—but staying the same will bankrupt your soul."

When I first began the journey of healing and stepping into my full power, no one warned me about the grief. Everyone talked about the glow-up. The business. The blessings. The luxury. But no one said a word about the *loss*.

No one told me that parts of me would have to die.
That I'd have to unlearn behaviors that once helped me survive.
That I'd have to leave behind people I once believed I couldn't live without.

I thought I could elevate and stay the same.
I thought I could rise and still keep everyone comfortable.
I thought I could become *her*—the whole, healed, wealthy, joyful woman—and not lose a thing along the way.

But *becoming costs*.

Not money—though sometimes that too. But belief. Boundaries. Boldness.
It costs control. It costs the need to be liked. It costs silence.
And most of all, it costs the version of you that once made everyone else feel secure while you slowly disappeared inside yourself.

You Don't Become Her Without Burial

I buried the girl who smiled when she wanted to cry.
I buried the woman who overworked to feel valuable.
I buried the version of me who would rather be accepted than aligned.

35

It wasn't cruel. It was sacred. Because every burial became a rebirth.

I became a woman who says no without explanation.
Who rests without guilt.
Who trusts her intuition even when it disrupts the plan.

That kind of woman doesn't arrive gently. She is *forged*.

Through fire. Through isolation. Through days of wondering if the price is too high — and still deciding to pay it.

I've missed out on invitations.
I've been talked about by people I once called family.
I've walked into rooms where I no longer fit.

But in every moment of discomfort, I remembered: *God is not building the woman I was. She's building the woman I'm becoming.*

Becoming Her Means Losing Who You Were — and Who They Needed You to Be

The truth is, some friendships didn't survive my becoming.
Not because I was cruel. But because I stopped playing the role they were used to.

I was no longer the one who could be called at any hour to carry their pain while ignoring mine.
I was no longer shrinking my voice to protect fragile egos.
I was no longer choosing peace at the expense of my truth.

And that made some people uncomfortable.

But here's the hard truth: *you can't become who you're meant to be and still maintain relationships rooted in your unhealed self.*

I remember one friend telling me I had changed — and she didn't mean it as a compliment.
I smiled and said, *"Thank you."* Because I had.

And the old me would've rushed to explain. Would've softened her shine. Would've apologized.
But the new me — the healed me — didn't owe anyone an explanation for her evolution.

If your growth threatens someone, they were never clapping for you — they were clapping for your compliance.

You Will Mourn the Familiar

There's grief in outgrowing people and places. There's grief in walking away from roles that once made you feel needed. There's grief in realizing you don't recognize your reflection — and at the same time, you've never felt more like yourself.

I cried over the woman I was leaving behind.
She fought hard. She survived storms with no umbrella. She carried children and trauma and dreams too heavy for one person to hold.
She deserved a thank you, a funeral, and a crown.

But she could not come with me.

Because healing demands honesty.
And honesty demands distance from what once felt like home.

Becoming Her Means Rewriting the Rules

I used to think I had to earn rest.
That success had to come with suffering.
That I had to overdeliver, overgive, and overlook my own needs just to prove I deserved a seat at the table.

Now I build my own tables — and sometimes I sit at them alone.
But the peace? It's unmatched.

I no longer contort myself to be digestible.
I no longer water myself down to be "nice."
I no longer confuse loyalty with bondage.

Becoming her means giving yourself *permission*.
To be seen. To be soft. To be successful.
To take up space, charge what you're worth, and trust your gut.

She Is Not Just a Dream—She Is the Blueprint

Becoming her meant more than new habits. It meant a new *identity*.

I began to see myself as a woman worthy of luxury, love, and leisure.
A woman who could build wealth and walk away from chaos without guilt.
A woman who didn't just inspire others—but led herself first.

That kind of woman doesn't just arrive — she is *built* from the inside out.
And once you meet her, you can't go back to pretending you don't know her.

She's not a fantasy.
She's not a Pinterest board.
She's not a trend.

She's your **becoming**. And she is you.

The more I honored her, the less I apologized.
The more I trusted her, the more things aligned.
The more I embodied her, the more I attracted divine partnerships, wealth, and purpose.

This wasn't manifestation. This was *maturity*.

Not Everyone Will Understand Your Becoming — And That's Okay

The higher I rose, the more misunderstood I became.
People asked, *"Who does she think she is?"*
The answer? *Everything God said I was.*

There is always a cost to becoming the version of yourself who no longer fits in survival spaces. But there is also freedom in no longer needing validation to breathe fully.

I stopped explaining.
I stopped softening my language.
I stopped editing my testimony to make others comfortable.

Because the truth is — if you want the power, you have to tell the full story.
The pain. The pivot. The price.

Legacy Over Likeness

I'm no longer here to be liked.
I'm here to be *remembered*.

When my grandchildren tell my story, I want them to know I was the woman who broke the curse. Who changed the game. Who cried and still led. Who got tired and still rose. Who prayed bold, invested wisely, and walked with God like she *knew* Her personally.

This version of me didn't come cheap.

She cost me my old beliefs.
She cost me relationships I thought I needed.
She cost me the comfort of invisibility.

But what I gained?

Peace.
Power.
Purpose.
And the *unshakeable knowing* that I was never created to stay small.

She Is Not Just a Dream—She Is the Blueprint

Becoming her meant more than new habits. It meant a new *identity*.

I began to see myself as a woman worthy of luxury, love, and leisure.
A woman who could build wealth and walk away from chaos without guilt.
A woman who didn't just inspire others—but led herself first.

That kind of woman doesn't just arrive — she is *built* from the inside out.

And once you meet her, you can't go back to pretending you don't know her.

She's not a fantasy.
She's not a Pinterest board.
She's not a trend.

She's your **becoming**. And she is you.

The more I honored her, the less I apologized.
The more I trusted her, the more things aligned.
The more I embodied her, the more I attracted divine partnerships, wealth, and purpose.

This wasn't manifestation. This was *maturity.*

Not Everyone Will Understand Your Becoming — And That's Okay

The higher I rose, the more misunderstood I became.
People asked, *"Who does she think she is?"*
The answer? *Everything God said I was.*

There is always a cost to becoming the version of yourself who no longer fits in survival spaces. But there is also freedom in no longer needing validation to breathe fully.

I stopped explaining.
I stopped softening my language.
I stopped editing my testimony to make others comfortable.

Because the truth is — if you want the power, you have to tell the full story.
The pain. The pivot. The price.

Reflection

- Where have you been dimming your light to keep others comfortable?
- What version of yourself are you afraid to release — even though she's outlived her purpose?
- What would it feel like to fully become the woman you've always known you were called to be?

Be honest. Becoming her costs. But so does staying stuck.

Affirmation

I honor who I've been.
I release who I no longer need to be.
I am becoming her — bold, whole, powerful, and free.
The price was high, but so am I — risen and radiant in my becoming.

Prayer: For Strength to Become Her

Dear God,
Thank You for never giving up on the woman I'm becoming —
even when I tried to hold on to the one I used to be.
Thank You for the grace to grow, even when growth felt lonely.
Give me the courage to release what's no longer aligned.
Let me walk boldly into my next chapter — unapologetic,
unshaken, and rooted in truth.
Show me how to love myself at every level.
Help me carry my becoming with dignity, softness, and divine
fire.I trust You. I trust the process. I trust *her.*
Amen.

Chapter 6: The Beauty of Building Slowly

"You're not behind. You're becoming."

We live in a world addicted to speed.
Faster success.
Faster money.
Faster healing.
Faster everything.

But the soul doesn't move on a deadline. The soul moves on
rhythm — on sacred, divine timing that can't be rushed no matter
how loudly the world demands results.

In my early days of building, I didn't understand that.
I was in survival mode. I thought *urgency was excellence.*
I wanted results yesterday. I felt behind before I even began. I
measured my worth by how quickly I could accomplish something.

When the vision for my legacy landed in my spirit, I sprinted.
I wanted the fruit without the root.
The influence without the infrastructure.
The platform without the process.

And like many women fueled by trauma and unhealed urgency, I
hit a wall.

Burnout.
Confusion.
Disappointment.
Loss of clarity.

I realized I wasn't building something sustainable — I was
building something *loud.*
But loud doesn't mean lasting. And God wasn't impressed with my
pace. God was inviting me to pause.

And in that pause, I heard it for the first time:

"You're not late. You're just in alignment."

Sacred Things Don't Get Rushed

Some of the most precious things in life take time:

- A baby in the womb.
- A tree taking root.
- A soul learning how to feel safe again.

I looked at my vision differently after that.
I no longer wanted quick success — I wanted **fruitful, faithful,** *generational* success.

And fruitful things are not rushed — they're *nurtured.*

That shift changed everything.
I started moving slower, but more intentionally.
I began checking in with my peace instead of just my progress.
I stopped working out of panic and started building from a place of power.

And power that's not rooted in peace is just performative.

The more I slowed down, the more clarity came.
The more I rested, the more creativity flowed.
The more I honored my body, my energy, and my emotional truth
— the more aligned my actions became.

This wasn't laziness. This was *spiritual strategy.*

Small Wins Are Still Wins

There was a time when I only celebrated big milestones.
The new car. The business launch. The big check.
But now? I celebrate everything.
Getting out of bed when I wanted to disappear.
Paying a bill in full.
Saying no without guilt.
Choosing rest instead of another late-night hustle session.

Because building slowly taught me that *small wins build sturdy foundations*.

Every prayer whispered in exhaustion.
Every page written while the kids napped.
Every budget adjusted to save just a little more.

They all mattered.

Success is not one giant leap. It's a thousand little choices no one clapped for.

And the truth is, the more I honored the small, the more God could trust me with the big.
Because slow builders don't just chase results — they *become* the kind of woman who can sustain them.

Sometimes You Need a Divine Recalibration

One of the most misunderstood parts of building slowly is that it *feels* like delay — when it's actually divine redirection.

I had seasons where everything paused.
Clients dried up.
Motivation disappeared.
Ideas that once flowed suddenly felt stuck.

I panicked.
I questioned the vision.
I asked God, *"Did I mess this up?"*

But what I learned is this: **sometimes God slows you down not to punish you — but to prepare you.**

Because you don't just need more income. You need more *capacity*.

You don't just need opportunities. You need wisdom to discern the *right* ones.

You don't just need growth. You need grounding.

And grounding doesn't happen in chaos.
It happens in quiet.
In stillness.
In the soft, sacred pauses where God reminds you:

"This isn't a setback. It's a setup. Let Me build you while you build it."

Redefining What It Means to Be Productive

There's a version of me that thought productivity meant doing everything, every day, at maximum speed.
But building slowly taught me something sacred:

Productivity isn't how much you do — it's how aligned your actions are with what matters.

Some of the most productive days I've had didn't involve checking off a to-do list.
They looked like:

- Sitting in silence and receiving clarity.
- Taking a walk to regulate my nervous system.
- Writing one *meaningful* page instead of forcing ten empty ones.

The world told me I had to hustle.
But Heaven whispered, *"Build in rhythm with Me."*

When I honored that, I became *more effective* — not less.
My work had more depth. My ideas were clearer. My energy was protected.
I wasn't stretched thin — I was *strategically poured out.*

I learned to honor my energy, my cycles, my body's wisdom.
I stopped making burnout the goalpost and started making **peace the measure** of success.

You Don't Have to Keep Up — You Just Have to Keep Going

Slow progress is still *divine progress.*

And maybe you're not behind — maybe you're just being **rooted**.
So that when the wind comes, you won't fall.
So that when the blessings pour in, you won't drown.
So that when you rise, it will be for real — not just for show.

I stopped comparing my path to women who were racing through theirs.
Because we're not even building the same thing.
Some people are building for applause. I'm building for **legacy**.
Some people are building for now. I'm building for my *children's children.*

And legacy takes time.

So I breathe deeper. I plan slower. I move with reverence.
Because I'd rather build what lasts than chase what's loud.

Healing Time Trauma

Time trauma is real.

It's what happens when your body remembers all the seasons you
ran out of time.
When you had deadlines, bills, kids crying, and no one to help.
When you rushed through healing because you had mouths to feed.
When you silenced your needs because survival left no room for
softness.

And now—even when you're no longer in survival mode—your
nervous system still operates like you are.

You wake up feeling behind.
You finish one task and already feel guilty for not doing the next.
You can't rest without thinking of what hasn't been done.

That's time trauma.

And slow building became my way of *healing* that trauma.

It reminded me:

You are not behind.
You are not lazy.
You are not unworthy because you move differently.

You are healing a timeline that was never yours to carry.
You are rewriting what urgency means.
You are telling your body the truth: *You are safe now.*

Rest Is Not a Reward — It's a Requirement

I used to believe I had to earn my rest.
That I had to work myself to the bone before I was allowed a nap,
a bath, a moment to breathe.

But God did not design me to burn out for a breakthrough.
God designed me to *build and rest.*
To *work and worship.*
To *plant and pause.*

I realized: rest is holy.
And rest isn't just sleeping — rest is **trusting.**

It's believing that if I take my hands off it for a moment, the vision
won't collapse.
That God is still working even when I am still.

Rest is a declaration of faith.
It says: I trust the process. I trust the pace. I trust that I don't have
to prove anything to be worthy of joy.

Divine Timing Is Still On Time

Sometimes I'd look around and wonder why it was taking so long.
Why other women were launching faster, scaling quicker, reaching
milestones I hadn't yet touched.

But I had to remember: *I wasn't building what they were building.*

I wasn't constructing a highlight reel.
I wasn't chasing followers or virality.
I was laying the foundation of a legacy that would stretch for generations.

That kind of vision takes time.
That kind of assignment requires *delay* — not as punishment, but as preparation.

God was never trying to slow me down to frustrate me —
She was slowing me down to **fortify** me.

To sharpen my discernment.
To strengthen my core.
To mature my money mindset.
To refine the *woman* before elevating the *work*.

Divine timing isn't about delay. It's about alignment.

When you surrender to it, you realize: nothing is missing.
Nothing is late.
Nothing is wasted.

You're not stuck. You're *being seasoned*.
You're not behind. You're *becoming*.

Reflection

- Where in your life have you been rushing through the process out of fear?
- What would it look like to trust the pace of your own path?
- In what ways can you honor the slow, sacred seasons of building instead of resisting them?

Affirmation

I am not behind. I am in alignment.
Every step I take is building something lasting, rooted, and holy.
I trust divine timing. I honor my own rhythm.
I am building a legacy — slowly, beautifully, and powerfully.

Prayer: For Peace in the Process

God who exists outside of time —
Thank You for reminding me that I don't have to rush to be
relevant.
I release the pressure to keep up. I surrender the lie that I'm
behind.
Help me fall in love with the process — not just the promise.
Let me trust the pauses as much as the progress.
Give me eyes to see the beauty in slow, sacred seasons.
Teach me that rest is holy, that peace is power, and that Your pace
is perfect.
I trust You with my timing. I trust You with my becoming.
Amen.

Chapter 7: Sacred Boundaries and Boss Moves

"Boundaries are not walls. They are invitations."

They invite people to meet you at the level of your healing, your peace, and your divine assignment.

But I didn't always know that.

In the early seasons of my grind, I thought "yes" was the language of love.
I said yes to emotional labor.
Yes to underpaying clients.
Yes to people who were more invested in my availability than my well-being.

I thought if I said yes enough, I'd finally be seen.
Finally be chosen.
Finally be safe.

But let me tell you what I learned the hard way:
Busyness without boundaries is not purpose — it's a trauma response.

I was over-functioning to avoid being abandoned.
I was overgiving to feel worthy.
I was overexplaining because deep down, I didn't believe my needs were valid on their own.

And it took breakdowns — sleepless nights, missed opportunities, even health scares — for me to realize this truth:

Boundaries aren't selfish. Boundaries are sacred.

Every "Yes" I Gave Others Was a "No" to Myself

I had to learn that every unspoken boundary is an open invitation to burnout.

I was trying to be a good friend, a good daughter, a good mom, a good businesswoman — and I thought that meant being available at all times. But it wasn't love. It was martyrdom.

And martyrdom is not sustainable.

I finally asked myself: *What would it look like to love myself the way I loved everyone else?*

So I started setting boundaries.

At first, I whispered them.
I apologized for them.
I gave disclaimers and softened the language.

But eventually — I started saying "no" like I meant it.

And here's what happened:
My **peace** increased.
My **purpose** clarified.
My **income** multiplied.

Because boundaries create **capacity.** And capacity creates **clarity.**

Clarity Always Comes With a Cost

Once I got clear on who I was and what I was building, not everyone celebrated.

Some people started falling back.
Others got offended.
Some assumed I thought I was "too good."

And for a moment, I questioned myself.
I asked, *Am I being too cold? Too distant? Too full of myself?*

But I realized — I wasn't being full of myself.
I was finally *being full of truth.*

Truth that said I deserve rest.
Truth that said I'm not available for disrespect.
Truth that said I don't negotiate my peace for the comfort of others.

Clarity costs comfort.
But comfort will cost you your calling if you cling to it too long.

So I stopped apologizing for being clear.
Clear about what I allow in my space.
Clear about my standards.
Clear about what alignment feels like in my body.

And I stopped letting guilt manipulate me out of obedience.

When They Push Back, Keep Standing

When you start enforcing boundaries, don't be surprised when people push back — especially if they were benefitting from your lack of them.

People will say you've changed (you have).
They'll say you're distant (you're protecting your energy).
They'll say you're acting brand new (because you *are* new — renewed, refocused, and finally free).

Here's what I want you to remember:

People who love you will adjust to your healing.
People who were using you will resist your healing.

Boundaries don't ruin real relationships — they *reveal* them.

And the more you stand firm in what honors your soul, the more room God has to send people who *actually respect you* — not just what you provide.

Boss Moves Require Emotional Boundaries

The moment I began to truly elevate as a boss mom was the moment I realized:
I'm not just building a business — I'm building a standard.

And that meant setting **emotional boundaries in business**.

No more explaining my prices.
No more over-delivering just to feel worthy.
No more saying yes to "collaborations" that drained my energy but filled someone else's pockets.

I stopped operating from people-pleasing and started operating from *positioning.*

Boss moves require emotional discipline.
You cannot take everything personally.
You cannot answer every call.
You cannot make every client's emergency your crisis.

I had to become the woman who could:

- Walk away from misaligned money
- Say no to good ideas in order to protect great ones
- Prioritize peace over people-pleasing

Because real boss moves are rooted in **strategy and sovereignty** — not stress.

Protecting Your Wealth Begins With Boundaries

If I wanted to grow wealth, I had to learn to **guard the gates**.

My time.
My inbox.
My calendar.
My team.
My contracts.

I no longer allowed "energy leaks" to cost me money.

When your boundaries are weak, your business bleeds.
When your standards are low, your stress is high.
When your identity isn't solid, you'll attract confusion — not clients.

So I got clear:

- Clear on my mission
- Clear on my offer
- Clear on my value
- Clear on the kind of clients who could walk with me — and the kind who could not

And when I stood firm, God honored it.
The right opportunities flowed.
The right partnerships emerged.
The right people *respected the price* — because I finally respected myself.

Legacy Requires Higher Standards

I'm not just setting boundaries for myself — I'm setting them for my lineage.

My children are watching how I lead.
They're learning how to navigate relationships.
They're studying how I respond to pressure, how I protect peace, how I walk away when something costs too much emotionally, spiritually, or energetically.

So I made a decision:

If it doesn't honor my legacy, it doesn't get my energy.

I no longer take calls from chaos.
I no longer answer messages that shake my peace.
I no longer explain basic respect.

Because I'm not building for the moment — I'm building for the *mantle.*

And the mantle requires maturity.

Your Energy Is a Sacred Assignment

You are not just a woman.
You are a vessel. A portal. A blueprint. A reflection of divine possibility.

Which means your energy is not casual — it's *consecrated.*

Protecting it is not an option. It's a spiritual act.

I had to stop entertaining conversations that left me drained.
Stop justifying access to people who hadn't earned it.
Stop "checking in" with people who only call when they want something.

Boundaries became my spiritual armor.
They became the way I told the world — and myself — *I matter.*

When you start honoring your energy like the sacred force it is, everything in your life shifts.

Doors close.
Favors dry up.
Old habits rise to tempt you.
But stay the course.

Because on the other side of discipline is *divine overflow.*

Reflection

- Where in your life have you been saying "yes" out of guilt instead of alignment?
- What relationships or patterns have been silently draining your energy?
- What would it look like to fully protect your peace, your power, and your purpose — without apology?

Affirmation

I protect my peace like it's sacred — because it is.
I no longer shrink to make others comfortable.
My boundaries are not walls — they are doors to my next level.
I lead with clarity. I speak with power. I build with boldness.
I am not for everyone — I am for alignment.
And that is more than enough.

Prayer: For Bold Boundaries and Elevated Leadership

God of divine order and holy wisdom,
Thank You for teaching me how to lead with clarity.
Thank You for reminding me that boundaries are love in action —
not rejection.
Give me the courage to say no without guilt.
Give me the discernment to know what is mine to carry and what
is not.
Let every "yes" I give be rooted in alignment, not fear.
Surround me with people who respect my voice, honor my energy,
and celebrate my healing.
Make me bold. Make me wise. Make me holy in my boundaries
and fearless in my becoming.
Amen.

Chapter 8: The Tools That Built Me

"I didn't have everything — but I used everything I had."

Let them tell it, I came up lucky.
Let them tell it, I always had the answers, the drive, the connections.
Let them tell it, I must've had someone behind the scenes guiding me.

But here's the truth:

I built my life with borrowed grace, divine grit, and tools nobody saw.

I didn't have startup capital.
I didn't have generational wealth.
I didn't have safety nets or big-name mentors.

I had prayer.
I had late nights and early mornings.
I had instincts. I had hunger. I had three kids depending on me.
And I had a non-negotiable truth in my bones: **This life was going to be different.**

Not just for me.
For them.
For my daughters. For their children. For every woman who came after me.

This chapter is not about cute apps or business hacks.
This is about the sacred, raw, real **tools that built me.**

Some I discovered in therapy.
Some I inherited through trial.
Some were handed to me by God in seasons I thought would destroy me.

And every single one has made me unshakable.

• Prayer & Discernment

Before I ever had a plan, I had prayer.
Prayer was my strategy when I didn't have solutions.
It was my clarity when everything around me was chaotic.
It was the compass I used to navigate betrayal, poverty, single motherhood, and purpose.

I didn't always know what to say — but I always knew who to go to.

Prayer built my discernment. And discernment saved my life.

I learned to stop asking everyone else what to do and instead sit still until I could *hear God for myself.*
Sometimes it came as a whisper.
Sometimes as a gut feeling.
Sometimes as a straight-up "no" when I was about to force a "yes."

Prayer taught me that peace is more powerful than proof.
Discernment showed me that every open door isn't divine — some are distractions in disguise.

This tool didn't just guide me — it matured me.
It kept me from signing bad contracts.
It revealed hidden motives.
It elevated my intuition into a weapon of wisdom.

And it reminded me that I wasn't doing this alone.
Even on my worst day, I was *spiritually backed.*

• Therapy & Self-Healing

There was a time I thought being strong meant never crying.
Never asking for help.
Never falling apart — at least not where anyone could see me.

But holding it all in made me heavy.
And I realized one day that I wasn't just tired — I was
traumatized.

Therapy gave me language for the pain I had normalized.

It gave me space to process years of survival.
It helped me unpack abandonment wounds, burnout cycles, and
why I was always trying to earn love through overgiving.

Some days I walked into those sessions numb.
Other days I cried through the entire hour.
But every time, I left lighter.

I began to heal the younger version of me — the girl who was
never protected.
The girl who learned to hustle before she learned to rest.
The girl who kept choosing people who didn't choose her back.

And I stopped asking, *"Why am I like this?"*
Instead, I started asking, *"What happened to me?"*

Self-healing isn't selfish. It's strategic.

It doesn't just free you — it frees your lineage.
The moment I chose to heal, I was choosing softness.
Peace.
Power.
Legacy.

This tool made me whole — not perfect, not polished — but
whole.

• Financial Literacy & Discipline

I didn't grow up with a financial education.
I grew up with struggle, with stretching, with making it work on fumes.
So when I entered the military, money felt like my first real taste of stability.
Regular paychecks. Housing. A system.

But even with that structure, I had no roadmap.
I knew how to survive — but I didn't know how to *build*.

The military taught me order, chain of command, accountability — but it didn't teach me how to create wealth.

I was disciplined in duty but scattered with dollars.
If I got paid on the 1st, it was gone by the 3rd.
If something broke down, it became a crisis.
There was no savings. No investment plan. No long-term vision.

I had to rewire everything I thought I knew about money.

And I started by getting honest.

- I stopped pretending I was "doing fine."
- I looked at the numbers.
- I tracked every dollar.
- I faced my fear of not having enough — and started making a plan to *have more than enough.*

I studied the wealthy.
I read the books.
I opened a savings account and committed to adding to it weekly — no matter how small the amount.

Financial literacy became a form of warfare — against lack, against fear, against generational silence.

Eventually, I got strategic:

- Cut back unnecessary spending
- Invested in tools that made me money back
- Repaired my credit
- Paid off debts in order of interest rate, not emotion

And the discipline I learned in the military?
It became a powerful partner.

Because now I had both **structure** and **strategy**.

I didn't just want to make money.
I wanted to *multiply it.*
I wanted to leave behind something more than just memories — I wanted to leave behind *momentum.*

• Hustle & Creative Income

When people say "I had to get it out the mud," I know exactly what they mean.
There were seasons where I didn't have options — I had *urgency.*
Rent was due. The fridge was low. My babies needed things I couldn't put off until payday.
So I got creative.

I sold gently used items on Poshmark.
I picked up shifts with Uber and Lyft.
I sold baked goods during the holidays.
I flipped what I had into what I needed.

Hustle wasn't just a badge of honor — it was survival in motion.

But I refused to stay there.
Because I knew hustle was a **bridge**, not a destination.

And I was determined not to die on the same bridge I was supposed to cross.

Over time, I stopped asking, *"What can I sell?"* and started asking, *"What do I know that others will pay to learn?"*

I began monetizing:

- My parenting wisdom
- My military background and time management skills
- My gift for writing and storytelling
- My natural eye for branding, beauty, and building emotional connection

And I learned that **income loves intention.**

When I stopped working from panic and started working from *purpose,*
my income shifted.

I built multiple streams not from luxury — but from *leverage.*

And each hustle became a seed that grew into a harvest I could finally rest in.

I wasn't just working anymore.
I was *designing freedom* — one creative move at a time.

• **Time Stewardship**

I used to feel like time was my enemy.
There was never enough of it.
Between work, motherhood, side hustles, and survival — I was constantly in a race against the clock.
And I was losing.

Until I realized something life-altering:

I didn't need *more* time — I needed to start *mastering* the time I had.

That's when I found books like *The 5 AM Club* and *The Miracle Morning*.
And for the first time, I began to understand the *spiritual power of routine*.

Waking up earlier didn't just give me more hours — it gave me **ownership** over my day.
That quiet time before the world started spinning gave me a window to breathe, think, plan, pray, and *reset*.

I started waking up with **intention**, not anxiety.
I created a rhythm:

- Prayer and silence before picking up my phone
- Journaling and vision casting
- Affirmations that reminded me of my power
- Reading to nourish my mind
- Stretching or walking to move my body into alignment

This wasn't just a productivity hack.
It was *spiritual preparation*.

Time stewardship taught me that how I start my day determines how I live my life.

I stopped multitasking and started **prioritizing.**
I created time blocks instead of to-do lists.
I scheduled peace just like I scheduled appointments.
And I gave myself permission to *rest* without guilt — because burnout is not a badge of honor.

As a mom, a builder, a visionary — I needed time to work *for* me, not just fly *past* me.

And now, instead of feeling like time is slipping away,
I feel like I'm finally *in sync* with it — honoring it, partnering with it, stewarding it like the divine resource it truly is.

• Community & Mentorship

There's a version of me that used to say, *"I got it."*
Even when I didn't.
Even when I was falling apart.

Because for so long, being strong meant being **alone**.

But truth be told, isolation almost took me out.
I was pouring into everyone else — and nobody was pouring back.
I was building legacies and holding space — with nobody holding me.

Until one day, I heard God whisper:

"Even Moses needed help to hold up his arms."

That's when I began praying for **true community**.
Not just people to network with — but people who could *see me* in the spirit.
Not just mentors with money — but mentors with *wisdom*.
Not just friends to talk to — but *covenant connections* who could speak life into my vision when I got weary.

I learned to lean into:

- Sisterhood over competition
- Spiritual leadership over performance
- Mutual support over one-sided loyalty
- Conversations that fed my purpose, not just my ego

I began asking better questions:

- Do they celebrate my growth or feel threatened by it?
- Can they hold me accountable with love?
- Do they call out the greatness in me — or the gossip around me?

The right community doesn't just cheer you on — they *protect your becoming.*

Mentorship became a mirror.
It showed me blind spots.
It helped me skip mistakes I didn't need to make.
It affirmed my gifts before the world ever noticed them.

Now I don't just build with hustle — I build with *help.*

And I no longer feel guilty for needing people.
I feel *wise* for making sure I'm no longer building alone.

• Systems & Structure

For years, I was doing *everything* by hand.
Following up manually.
Creating things from scratch.
Staying up late responding to messages, sending invoices, organizing documents.
Winging it — but making it look polished.

But behind the scenes?
I was exhausted.

Until I had a breakdown that turned into a breakthrough.
I realized I wasn't tired from building — I was tired from doing things that could have been **automated** or **delegated**.

Systems saved my sanity.

I began to treat my brand like a business — not just a hustle.
I created:

- Email templates that answered FAQs in seconds
- Automated booking and payment systems
- Client intake forms
- Scheduling apps that synced with my calendar
- Brand kits, folders, and digital workflows

Every small automation freed up emotional and creative energy.
Every piece of structure became a form of self-respect.

I stopped trading peace for productivity.
I stopped earning every dollar with sweat — and started earning some with strategy.

Structure didn't make me robotic — it made me *powerful.*
It made space for motherhood, for rest, for soul work, for play.

And when I finally had systems in place, something beautiful happened:
I stopped panicking.
I stopped apologizing.
I stopped operating from urgency and started leading with *ease.*

Systems didn't just organize my work — they organized *my life.*

Now when people ask how I do it all, I smile.
Because the truth is:

I don't do it all — I **designed it all** to support me.

• **Faith & Favor**

There were some doors that didn't open because I knocked.
They opened because *God broke the lock.*

There were some moments I didn't qualify on paper —
But I was chosen anyway.

That wasn't luck.
That was **favor**.

Faith was the currency I used before money ever showed up.
Favor was the open hand of Heaven on places I hadn't even prayed
for yet.

There were times I showed up to the interview underdressed.
Times I launched the offer without a funnel.
Times I sat in meetings nervous, unsure, overthinking my worth.
And still, the *yes* came.
The contract was signed.
The resource appeared.
The connection was made.

Because I wasn't moving alone.
I was *carried.*

My faith taught me to keep walking, even when I couldn't see the
finish line.
It taught me that God's plan was often bigger than my preparation.

I stopped asking, *"How will it happen?"*
And I started saying, *"God, do what only You can do."*

And God did.

He multiplied my time.
He increased my income.
He expanded my capacity.
He put my name in rooms I hadn't entered yet.

And He protected me from opportunities that weren't aligned —
even when I begged for them.

Faith is the tool that kept me going.
Favor is the tool that took me further than I imagined.

And together?
They became a divine business strategy that no algorithm could
ever replicate.

• Bonus Tools: The Quiet Things That Built Me

Not every tool that built me was loud.
Not all of them were shiny.
Some of the most powerful tools came wrapped in stillness,
struggle, or solitude.
They didn't announce themselves — but they *refined* me.

Here are the ones that rarely get celebrated, but made all the
difference:

• Boundaries
Saying "no" felt like betrayal at first.
But boundaries taught me that self-abandonment isn't loyalty.
It's self-neglect.

I learned to protect my peace like a paycheck.
I stopped overexplaining.
I stopped making space for people who drained me.
And I realized — the more I respected my "no," the more powerful
my "yes" became.

• Silence

The world loves noise.
But silence taught me how to *hear* God, and more importantly,
how to hear *myself.*

I unplugged to reconnect.
I stopped filling every empty space with distraction.
And in the quiet, I found truth I would've missed in motion.

• Grief

Success has a strange way of revealing what never healed.
Every time I hit a new level, I had to grieve the version of me I
was leaving behind.
The one who accepted less.
The one who didn't know her worth.
The one who was praised for surviving but never asked if she was
okay.

Grief became a tool — not just for loss, but for *release.*

• Forgiveness

I had to forgive people who never apologized.
I had to forgive the version of me who didn't know better.
And I had to forgive the world for making Black motherhood so
hard, so invisible, so heavy.

Forgiveness became the tool that kept my hands open.
So I could receive everything God had for me.

• Joy

I used to wait for joy.
Now I create it.

I dance in the kitchen.
I celebrate small wins.
I light candles even when no one's coming over.
I laugh with my children.
I take photos I never post.
Joy became my rebellion.
Joy became my *reward*.

These weren't just survival tools — they were soul tools.
And every one of them helped build a woman no storm could shake.

Reflection

- What tools have you used in silence, without applause, that shaped who you are today?
- Are there tools you've overlooked because they didn't look "successful" enough on the outside?
- What inner resource are you finally ready to trust and lean into more deeply?
- Which part of you is asking to be re-equipped with fresh strategy, healing, or divine support?

Affirmation

I am built from wisdom, not just willpower.
I honor the tools I've used, both seen and unseen.
Nothing I've walked through has been wasted.
Everything has shaped my strength.
I release shame about my beginnings.
I rise, fully resourced — spiritually, emotionally, mentally, and financially.

I don't just survive anymore.
I build. I heal. I lead. I overflow.
Because I am the woman who uses what she has, and becomes
more than anyone imagined.

Prayer: For Divine Resourcefulness and Peaceful Power

God of provision, strategy, and sacred timing —
Thank You for every tool You placed in my hands,
even when I didn't recognize them as divine.
Thank You for giving me discernment when I wanted direction,
for rest when I wanted results,
and for stillness when I begged for signs.

Remind me that I lack nothing.
That I am never empty — only evolving.
Anoint my hands to build wisely.
Anoint my mind to see creatively.
Anoint my time to produce legacy, not just labor.
Teach me to trust what You've already given me.
Surround me with divine connections, sacred systems, and wise
mentors.
Let every move I make be led by clarity and covered by grace.
In this season, I build not from survival — but from softness,
strategy, and strength.

Amen.

Chapter 9: Thriving Like a Boss

"Thriving is my birthright — not a bonus."

I didn't always know what it meant to thrive.
I knew what it meant to push.
To produce.
To survive.
To show up for everybody and everything — even when I had nothing left.

For years, I mastered the art of high-functioning pain.
I was productive, polished, and praised.
But I wasn't *present.*
I wasn't *peaceful.*
And deep down, I wasn't even sure I was safe enough to dream beyond my survival.

Then came the shift.
It didn't happen all at once.
But it was undeniable.

I started craving *ease.*
I started craving *joy that wasn't earned with exhaustion.*
I started craving a life where I wasn't just building for others — I was nourishing *myself.*

Thriving isn't just a higher level of hustling.
It's a *different frequency altogether.*

It's moving from urgency to alignment.
From lack to overflow.
From proving to *embodying.*

And when I say I'm thriving like a boss, I don't mean I have it all figured out.

I mean I *trust myself now*.
I rest without guilt.
I lead without shrinking.
I ask for what I need.
I protect my peace like it's sacred — because it is.

This chapter is my declaration that I made it through the war of womanhood, and I didn't just survive it — I *rewrote the rules*.

Welcome to the era of my thriving.
And welcome to the movement that was born from it.

• The Inner Shift: Redefining What Success Means

There comes a moment — maybe you've felt it too —
when success no longer feels like applause.
It doesn't feel like the paycheck, the promotion, or the performance.
It starts to feel like *peace*.

There was a time I chased everything that looked impressive.
I wanted the career growth, the recognition, the material markers that said, "She made it."
And I did get some of those things.
But here's what nobody talks about:

Achieving what you thought you wanted can still leave you empty if you're not aligned with your truth.

Sis, let me ask you:
Have you ever hit a goal — and felt a strange sadness afterward?
Have you ever done "the right thing" only to realize it wasn't *your* thing?

That's where the inner shift begins.

You start asking deeper questions:

- "What do I really want?"
- "Who am I when I'm not performing?"
- "What would it look like to thrive from a place of softness, not struggle?"

When I finally sat with those questions, I realized:
I didn't want to be impressive anymore.
I wanted to be **fulfilled**.
I didn't want to just make it — I wanted to make meaning.
I didn't want to lead from burnout — I wanted to lead from *overflow*.

Success used to be how others saw me.
Now it's how I *feel* when I look in the mirror.

And you, Boss Mom, are allowed to shift too.

You're allowed to reimagine what success looks like now.
You're allowed to say, "That served me once — but I've outgrown it."
You're allowed to crave something softer.
Something sacred.
Something *yours*.

Because when your definition of success changes, your *entire life starts to align with who you've become.*

• Boss Energy: Walking in Authority and Grace

There is a shift that happens — not when life gets easier, but when *you get clearer.*

You start showing up differently.

Not because you have all the answers.
Not because everything's perfect.
But because you finally know who you are, and you stop apologizing for it.

That's **Boss Energy**.

It's not loud, but it's undeniable.
It doesn't scream — it *settles*.
It walks into a room with peace and expects to be respected — not because of ego, but because of embodiment.

And sis, you have it.
Even if the world hasn't recognized it yet.
Even if your current life doesn't reflect your full vision.
The authority you're craving isn't out there — it's *already in you.*

Boss Energy is:

- Showing up in meetings and no longer minimizing your brilliance
- Saying "No, thank you" without a 3-paragraph explanation
- Choosing joy, even when you're still healing
- Wearing what you want, speaking how you speak, and commanding space without shrinking

It's the quiet confidence that says:
"I don't chase — I attract. I don't prove — I align. I don't beg — I build."

You don't need a title to be a boss.
You don't need a million followers, a six-figure income, or a perfect morning routine.

You need **clarity.**
You need **boundaries.**
You need a deep, sacred knowing that your power is *not performative — it's prophetic.*

And when you walk in that truth, people can feel it.
Your children feel it.
Your friends feel it.
Your clients feel it.

Because you're not just building a business or a brand.
You're walking in **Boss Energy** — and the world adjusts accordingly.

• The Power of Feminine Leadership

There's a reason you feel out of place in toxic workspaces.
There's a reason your body tightens when someone tells you to "man up" or "leave your emotions at the door."

Because you were never meant to lead like them.
You were meant to lead like *you*.

Boss Moms lead with intuition.
We lead with heart, with Spirit, with soul.
We create strategy *and* safety.
We build spaces where people don't just perform — they *belong*.

Feminine leadership isn't about being passive.
It's about being powerful in a way that feels whole.

It's:

- Creating from alignment, not anxiety
- Listening deeper before speaking louder
- Knowing when to rest, when to rise, and when to *redirect the entire room* without raising your voice
- Making your boundaries known without making your voice brittle
- Knowing that nurturing *is* a business strategy — one that builds loyalty, trust, and longevity

Sis, the world needs women who lead like this.

We've seen what happens when leadership lacks empathy.
We've watched generations of women burn out trying to lead like
men.
But you — you get to do it differently.

You get to lead with Divine guidance and *still be taken seriously*.
You get to walk into boardrooms with your curls out, your voice
firm, and your energy grounded — and not shrink for anyone.

And if someone calls you "too emotional," smile.
Because emotion is how we **feel the truth**.
And the truth is what changes everything.

You don't have to be harder to be heard.
You don't have to toughen up to take the lead.

You get to be *fully woman* — and still *fully boss*.

• No Longer Hiding: The Bold Decision to Take Up Space

For a long time, I thought being humble meant being small.
I thought success had to be quiet, private, polite.
I was afraid of being "too much."
Too loud.
Too confident.
Too visible.

But hiding didn't make me more holy.
It just made me **exhausted.**

Sis, can you relate?

Have you ever watered yourself down to be digestible for people
who weren't even for you?

Have you ever waited to post that idea, start that business, wear that outfit, or speak that truth — because you didn't want to make anyone uncomfortable?

That's not humility.
That's fear in a nice dress.
And it doesn't serve you.

Taking up space is not arrogance — it's *alignment.*

You were born to *be seen.*
You were born to be *heard.*
You were born to lead something, shape something, create something that only you can.

And I get it — being visible is vulnerable.
But hiding has a cost, too.
It costs you your voice.
Your opportunities.
Your joy.

I had to unlearn the belief that I needed to "earn" the right to be confident.
That I needed to *wait* until I was thinner, richer, more polished, more perfect.

No.
I stopped waiting.
I started walking.
And the moment I decided to *own the room I used to tiptoe in,* everything shifted.

Boss Moms take up space with love.
We lead with presence.
We shine — not to outshine others, but to remind them they can shine, too.

And sis, this is your moment.
No more hiding.
Take up *all* the space God made for you.

• Overflow Mindset: From Just Enough to More Than Enough

For too long, I lived in the land of "just enough."
Just enough energy to get through the day.
Just enough money to cover the bills.
Just enough peace to smile through the chaos.

I was surviving — but barely.
And I had normalized it.
I thought it was noble to get by on scraps.
To make miracles out of nothing.
To wear resilience like armor and never ask for *more*.

But then I had a revelation:

I serve a God of abundance.
So why was I still living like I needed to apologize for wanting more?

Sis, hear me clearly:
Wanting more is not greedy — it's **God-given.**

You weren't designed to live in emotional overdraft.
You weren't called to carry everyone else and never have enough left for yourself.

You are allowed to overflow.

Overflow looks like:

- Having peace that isn't tied to your productivity
- Saying yes to things that light you up instead of drain you

- Investing in your joy, your rest, your beauty — without guilt
- Having money in the bank *and* time to enjoy your life
- Pouring into others from a cup that's already full, not barely dripping

When I embraced overflow, I stopped making decisions from fear.
I started giving from wholeness, not obligation.
I stopped chasing the bare minimum and started expecting the best.

And let me say this to you as clearly as I can:
You don't have to earn rest.
You don't have to earn softness.
You don't have to prove your worth by how much you sacrifice.

You are worthy of more than enough.

Let go of the scarcity mindset.
Release the belief that being overworked is honorable.
Step boldly into overflow — because you deserve to live *blessed and balanced.*

• **The Legacy You're Creating**

Every decision you make as a Boss Mom isn't just about you —
it's about the future you're creating.
The seeds you're planting.
The cycles you're breaking.

Legacy isn't just money in a trust fund.
Legacy is **emotional wealth.**
Legacy is **healing.**
Legacy is a daughter who knows her worth,
and a son who respects a woman who walks in hers.

Sis, you are a generational shift.

When you choose softness over survival,
when you choose therapy over silence,
when you invest in your dreams instead of dismissing them —
you're rewriting what's possible for your bloodline.

And I know it's heavy sometimes.
I know you get tired of being the one who "gets it."
The one who is healing, holding, handling it all.

But look around — and look ahead.

Your children are watching you rise.
Your future grandchildren are receiving the fruit of your sacrifices
right now.
Your last name is being elevated through your *everyday choices.*

This is why we do the work.
This is why we build with intention.
Not just to thrive in the moment — but to create a *movement*
through our lineage.

You're creating a new normal where joy is regular.
Where wealth isn't rare.
Where softness is modeled.
Where freedom is expected — not just hoped for.

That's the real Boss Mom Effect.

It doesn't stop with your story.
It multiplies through your family, your community, and the women
who will rise because *you* did.

• The Boss Mom Effect as a Movement

When I started this journey, I was just trying to breathe.
Trying to make it.

Trying to figure out how to be a good mother, a whole woman, and a provider — without losing myself in the process.

But somewhere along the way, I realized I wasn't alone.
My story echoed in other women's voices.
In their inboxes.
In their silent prayers whispered over kitchen sinks and steering wheels.
In their strength... and in their sadness.

And that's when *The Boss Mom Effect* was born.

It wasn't about becoming a brand.
It was about giving language to a reality so many of us were living but never naming.

It's a movement rooted in **healing, hustling, and building wealth — on our terms.**

It's for the mom who's been overlooked, but never gave up.
For the woman who's balancing school drop-offs and speaking engagements.
For the entrepreneur who's creating magic between naptime and midnight.
For the ones who are exhausted but still *dreaming anyway.*

This movement says:

- You don't have to choose between motherhood and mission
- You can build wealth without becoming hard
- You can take up space, lead with softness, and still command the room
- You can heal what hurt you and still build something sacred

The Boss Mom Effect is a reminder that you're not behind — you're becoming.
And your becoming is *contagious.*

Every time you rise, you give someone else permission to do the same.
Every time you speak your truth, you make it safer for another woman to find hers.
Every time you choose alignment over approval, you shift the atmosphere for your whole bloodline.

This isn't just about business.
This is about **birthing a new standard.**

Boss Moms are builders, leaders, nurturers, and visionaries.
And we're done playing small.

We're not waiting to be chosen.
We've already claimed our space — and we're *filling it with purpose.*

• Mentoring the Next Woman: Giving Back and Building Community

I didn't get here alone.
And neither will the next woman.

There were women who poured into me —
with prayers, with wisdom, with hugs that said "You've got this,"
even when I wasn't sure I did.

Some of them had titles.
Most of them didn't.
But they all held keys that unlocked something in me.

And now, I hold keys too.

Being a Boss Mom isn't just about how far you climb.
It's about how many women you *lift* on the way.

There's a woman watching you right now.
She might be in your family.
She might be in your office, your DMs, your circle.
She might be your daughter.

She sees how you move.
She notices how you rest.
She hears what you say *and* what you no longer tolerate.

You are her permission slip.
Her blueprint.
Her quiet mentor.

And that's why I believe **community is wealth.**
Because you can't build a legacy in isolation.
You build it in sisterhood.
In late-night phone calls and voice notes that say "I believe in you."
In sharing what worked — and what didn't — so she doesn't have to start from scratch.

Boss Moms build differently.
We don't hoard knowledge.
We *pass it on.*

We start podcasts.
We coach other mothers.
We speak at events, launch platforms, create safe spaces.
Not because we want to be famous — but because we remember what it felt like to be invisible.

We are the ones who turn our becoming into *a bridge* for the next woman.

And maybe that's the highest form of thriving —
To rise,
and to reach.

Reflection

- What does thriving look like *for you* — not what you were taught, but what your soul needs?
- Where are you still playing small, even though you've outgrown the box?
- What belief do you need to let go of in order to lead like a Boss Mom?
- Who around you is waiting for you to rise — not perfectly, but powerfully?

Affirmation

I am not here to survive — I am here to *thrive*.
I lead with softness, power, and divine clarity.
I take up space without apology.
I pour from overflow, not obligation.
I am building legacy, birthing wealth, and walking in purpose.
I am a Boss Mom — and my becoming is a movement.
I don't just rise — I reach.
I don't just build — I multiply.
I am her. I choose her. I *honor* her.
Every single day.

Prayer: For the Woman Becoming Her Boldest Self

God of overflow and holy becoming —
Thank You for the woman reading these words.

Thank You for every storm she's survived,
every secret seed she's planted,
every moment she showed up when it would've been easier to
shrink.

Cover her with clarity.
Surround her with sisters who speak life.
Open doors no fear can close.
May her softness be her strength.
May her wisdom be her wealth.
May her rest be her reward.
And may her legacy echo louder than any limitation she's ever
faced.

Let her thrive in business, in motherhood, in marriage, in solitude
—
not from exhaustion, but from embodiment.
Let her remember she is not behind — she is *becoming*.

Amen.

Chapter 10: The Boss Mom Manifesto

"I am not who the world tried to make me — I am who God destined me to become."

There comes a moment when a woman stops asking for permission and starts writing her own rules.

When she stops just surviving motherhood and begins designing motherhood on *her terms.*

When she realizes that building wealth, healing her lineage, protecting her softness, and leading with wisdom aren't separate goals — they're all part of her divine assignment.

This chapter is not just a statement.
It's a **manifesto**.
It's for the woman who's felt unseen, uncelebrated, and underestimated — and is ready to rewrite the narrative.

If you're reading this, it's because you're that woman.
You're ready to take up space, not just as a mom, not just as a woman, but as a **Boss** — a divine architect of legacy, healing, and power.

Let this be your rally cry.

• I Build Without Apology

I am not asking anyone to validate my vision.

I don't need approval to dream.
I don't need a seat at the table — I *build the house.*
I create from purpose, not pressure.
And I no longer downplay my brilliance to make others comfortable.

I build businesses, homes, families, wealth, wellness, and peace —
because I was made for all of it.

• I Mother From Wholeness, Not Martyrdom

I release the need to perform perfection.
I refuse to parent from depletion.
I model healing, not hiding.
I teach rest, not just resilience.

My children don't just watch me serve — they watch me *rise.*
And in watching me rise, they are learning how to honor
themselves, too.

• I Protect My Softness As Sacred

I am no longer available for burnout disguised as responsibility.
I no longer accept chaos as normal.
I no longer feel guilty for resting, saying no, or walking away.

My softness is not a weakness — it's a *weapon.*
It is a form of power that makes room for joy, clarity, and sacred
alignment.

• I Am the Chain Breaker

The pain didn't start with me,
but the healing?
It starts right here.

I don't just carry burdens — I **transform** them.
I don't run from generational patterns — I confront them.

I'm not afraid to be the first in my family to say, "This ends with me."

I am not just my ancestors' wildest dream — I am their answered prayer.

And I don't carry guilt for thriving.
I carry **gratitude**.
Because thriving is how I honor them.
Thriving is how I build forward.

• I Do Not Lead Alone

I may walk with strength, but I don't walk in isolation.

I welcome support.
I ask for help without shame.
I build with women who get it.
I create with sisters who speak life, not competition.

Boss Moms don't believe in lack —
we believe in **legacy through community.**

If I rise, we rise.
If I win, we all eat.
And if I build, I leave the door open for the next one.

• I Make Money With Purpose and Power

Wealth is not just a goal — it is my **birthright**.

I don't chase money.
I attract aligned opportunity.
I invest wisely.

I give generously.
I budget with clarity.
I spend with joy.

Money doesn't own me — I own my mission.

And I no longer shrink my prices, my value, or my expectations for fear of being "too much."

Because money in the hands of a healed woman becomes a tool for transformation.

• I Am Not Behind — I Am Becoming

I reject the timelines that tell me I'm late.
I refuse to rush divine timing.
I trust the pace of my evolution.

Whether I am rebuilding, resting, reinventing, or rising —
I am always *becoming* more of who I truly am.

There is no missed window.
No wasted season.
No expiration on my purpose.

Every part of my journey was necessary.
And everything I desire is still on the way.

• I Show Up Fully

No more half-hearted energy.
No more smiling through suppression.
No more shrinking to keep the peace.

I show up fully — in every room, every role, every opportunity.
I bring my truth. My voice. My lived experience. My sacred "no."
I don't perform — I *embody.*

I trust that the right people, places, and platforms will rise to meet the *real* me.

• I Speak Life Over Myself

I am no longer waiting for others to affirm me.
I don't need the applause to know I'm worthy.
I am no longer fueled by proving — I'm rooted in knowing.

I speak life over myself, even when no one else does.
I am my own loudest cheerleader, my gentlest comfort, my firmest advocate.

I bless my body.
I bless my dreams.
I bless my bank account.
I bless my motherhood, my business, and my beautiful, bold journey.

• I Am the Blueprint

I am not imitating anyone — I *am* the model.
The way I move becomes the mirror someone else needs.
My story, my scars, my softness — they're not liabilities. They are *legacy.*

I am the example of what's possible.
I don't just break molds — I birth new ones.

I am not the exception — I am the **blueprint**.

• This Is My Era

I have grieved.
I have grown.
I have gathered myself.
And now? I rise.

This is my era of divine ease.
This is my era of aligned expansion.
This is my era of resting and receiving, not running and reaching.

I don't chase. I align.
I don't force. I flow.
I don't beg. I **become.**

This is my era —
and I will not apologize for how bright I shine in it.

Reflection

- What parts of this manifesto made you feel most seen?
- Where have you been dimming your light, and what would it look like to shine without apology?
- What outdated beliefs are you ready to release so you can build without guilt?
- What legacy are you building, not just for your children — but for *yourself*?

Affirmation

I am not a copy — I am the blueprint.
I am not behind — I am becoming.

I lead with softness, walk in power, and speak life over myself daily.
I honor my motherhood, protect my boundaries, and multiply wealth with wisdom.
I do not wait for doors — I build them.
I do not shrink for love — I expand in truth.
This is my era. I choose it boldly.
I am a Boss Mom — and my life is the legacy.

Prayer: For the Woman Who Is Ready to Lead Boldly

God of clarity and courage,
Bless this woman who is rising.
Bless her body, her vision, her mind, her money.
Bless the work of her hands and the softness of her heart.

Break every lie that tells her she is too late, too loud, too tired, too complicated.
Remind her that she is **exactly** who You called — for such a time as this.

Give her strength to walk away from what no longer serves her.
Give her peace that surpasses understanding — even in the middle of uncertainty.
Give her joy that cannot be shaken, and strategy that cannot be stolen.

Anoint her leadership, her home, her business, and her lineage.
May she rise not in fear, but in **fullness.**

Amen.

Chapter 11: Becoming Her Daily

"Becoming her once is powerful. Becoming her every day is where the real work begins."

You don't become a Boss Mom by accident.

You become her in the quiet hours.
In the daily choices no one applauds.
In the silent battles no one sees.
In the micro-decisions that multiply into transformation over time.

This chapter is not about chasing perfection — it's about **intentional embodiment.**

It's about waking up and choosing yourself before the world tries to define you.

It's about cultivating rhythm, not just routine.
Divine flow, not just forced productivity.

This is about *daily becoming* — and building a life that holds the woman you're still unfolding into.

• The Power of Ritual Over Routine

Routines create structure.
But rituals create **alignment**.

Routines tell your body where to go.
Rituals tell your soul who you are.

Every Boss Mom needs both.
But the magic happens when your calendar isn't just full — it's *intentional.*

Your morning is sacred space.
Not just time to "get ready," but time to **get rooted**.

Whether it's 5 minutes or 50, there's something holy about how you start the day:

- Reading Scripture or a devotion
- Whispering affirmations while brushing your teeth
- Sitting with tea and asking, "What do I need today?"
- Moving your body — not to punish it, but to *honor* it

Your rituals are your reminders.
They reconnect you to the highest version of yourself before the world has a chance to distract you.

You don't need a perfect morning — you need an **anchored one.**

• Time Stewardship, Not Time Management

Time management is about control.
Time stewardship is about *honor.*

You're not just managing minutes — you're stewarding your **purpose**.

This is where books like *The 5AM Club* and *The Miracle Morning* cracked something open in me.
They taught me that time is not just something to chase — it's something to *protect.*

Every hour you give to chaos is an hour stolen from your calling.

Your calendar isn't just a schedule — it's a **reflection of your values**.

Ask yourself:

- Where does my peace live on this calendar?
- Where does my healing have space?
- Where does legacy-building time for my goals exist — uninterrupted and sacred?

When you steward your time, you reclaim your *life*.

• Divine Feminine Habits

Masculine hustle says: push harder.
Divine feminine wisdom whispers: flow deeper.

Boss Moms don't abandon strategy — we pair it with **intuition**.
We understand our cycles, our emotional rhythms, our inner seasons.

Some days are for launching.
Some days are for nurturing.
Some days are for quiet — *and that, too, is powerful.*

Divine feminine habits might look like:

- Syncing your business calendar with your menstrual or lunar cycle
- Journaling not just goals, but *feelings*
- Scheduling your rest with the same priority as your meetings
- Allowing pleasure — beautiful food, soft clothes, fresh flowers — to be part of your day

This isn't laziness. This is **legacy in alignment.**
This is building without burnout.
This is softness as sacred strategy.

• Healing Rhythms & Rest

Boss Moms don't earn rest — we are *entitled* to it.

We are raising generations, creating wealth, healing trauma, navigating systemic stress, and showing up with style. Rest is not optional — it is **required.**

Healing rhythms are how we repair what the world tries to wear down.
They are how we keep our nervous systems soft and our boundaries strong.

These rhythms can be as simple as:

- Midday check-ins: "Where am I holding tension?"
- Weekly self-care sabbaths
- Sleep rituals: lavender oil, silk pillowcases, 30 minutes of quiet
- Mind-body healing: breathwork, therapy, movement, nature walks

Healing isn't a one-time thing. It's a rhythm — a *return* to yourself.

• Sacred Boundaries for Boss Moms

You can't pour from an empty well — but you also can't fill it if it keeps leaking.

Boundaries are not walls.
They are **sacred fences** that protect your garden.

Boss Mom boundaries might sound like:

- "I'm unavailable for that energy today."

- "I only take calls on Tuesdays."
- "I don't work after 6 PM because I'm with my children."
- "This is my rest day — I'll get back to you tomorrow."

And guess what?
You don't need to justify boundaries that protect your wellness.
You don't need to explain your *no* to people who benefited from your *yes*.

Boundaries are how Boss Moms teach the world how to treat them.

• Wealth Practices That Start Small

Daily becoming also looks like wealth stewardship — even in tiny steps.

Wealth isn't always about the big moves.
It's about the **small daily agreements** with your future self.

Boss Mom wealth practices might include:

- Transferring $20/week to an investment account
- Reading one chapter of a financial book a night
- Tracking spending from a place of curiosity, not shame
- Speaking wealth affirmations in the mirror every morning
- Having a money date with yourself each Friday — tea, music, and financial goals

You don't become wealthy overnight.
You become wealthy *on purpose.*
A Boss Mom builds wealth not just for herself — but for her children's children.

• Daily Words That Transform the Home

The energy of your home responds to your voice.

The words you speak over yourself, your children, and your space become **blueprints for belief.**

Try these simple, sacred phrases:

- "This home is a sanctuary."
- "I am the calm in the chaos."
- "We are safe, we are loved, we are blessed."
- "I bless my children with peace and power."
- "Money flows to me because I steward it wisely."
- "I honor the woman I am becoming."

Say them in the kitchen.
Say them in the mirror.
Say them in the car after a long day.

Your voice sets the spiritual temperature.
Speak like the woman you're becoming.

Reflection

- What daily habits help you feel like the most aligned, powerful version of yourself?
- Where have you been operating from burnout instead of balance?
- What small shift can you make tomorrow morning to reclaim your time, energy, or peace?
- What would it look like to live in rhythm with your body, spirit, and purpose?
- How do you want your children to remember the *energy* of your home?

Affirmation

I honor my rhythms.
I cherish my softness.
I steward my time with grace and clarity.
I show up daily for the woman I'm becoming — with love, not judgment.
I am not behind. I am aligned.
I choose peace. I protect joy. I plant seeds of wealth and wellness every day.
My habits hold my healing.
My rituals anchor my rising.
I am a Boss Mom — and I become her daily.

Prayer: For the Woman Who Is Learning to Be Gentle With Herself

God of grace and new beginnings,
Today I choose to come home to myself.

Teach me how to love the ordinary moments.
Teach me how to move in rhythm with what is holy and human inside of me.
Let me rise early not from fear of falling behind — but from joy in meeting myself.

Bless the hands that prepare meals, type emails, wipe tears, and build empires.
Bless the hours that feel thankless — and remind me they are not wasted.
Bless my morning rituals, my evening reflections, and all the space in between.

Let my daily becoming be a sacred act.
Let my small choices become big breakthroughs.

Let my softness remain intact, even in a world that tries to harden me.

I don't need to do it all today.
But I *will* do what aligns with the woman I'm becoming.
And that is more than enough.

Amen.

The Boss Mom Toolkit

"You are already her — but these tools will help you walk like her, lead like her, and build like her every single day."

This isn't just a toolkit. It's your reminder that wealth, healing, joy, and alignment are not out of reach — they're within your power. Inside you'll find the resources, habits, and wisdom that helped me rise, and now they're here to help you too.

Let's begin with your personal and professional foundation.

Wellness & Mental Health Support

Boss Moms can't pour from an empty vessel — here's how to refill it with intention:

- **Therapy Platforms**
  BetterHelp, Therapy for Black Girls, and local trauma-informed therapists can be lifelines.
- **Nervous System Regulation Tools**
  Breathwork (like The Breath Guy), EFT tapping, somatic body scans, and yoga nidra for deep restoration.
- **Mood-Boosting Essentials**
  - Magnesium & Ashwagandha

- o Walking barefoot in grass (grounding)
   - o Creating a "joy corner" at home filled with candles, quotes, and softness
- **Sleep Rituals**
  Silk pillowcases, blackout curtains, calming teas, and screen-free bedtime routines.

Your softness is sacred. Protect it like it's a million-dollar asset — because it is.

Books That Shifted Everything

These were more than books — they were *blueprints*:

- *The 5AM Club* by Robin Sharma — Time mastery through sacred morning rituals
- *The Miracle Morning* by Hal Elrod — Mornings that set the tone for wealth and wellness
- *Atomic Habits* by James Clear — Building systems that make success automatic
- *We Should All Be Millionaires* by Rachel Rodgers — Feminine leadership in finances
- *Sacred Woman* by Queen Afua — Divine feminine healing and ancestral alignment
- *Rich Dad Poor Dad* by Robert Kiyosaki — Understanding assets vs. liabilities

Don't just read to learn — read to become.

Apps That Make Boss Life Easier

Technology should support your peace — not overwhelm it. These tools help Boss Moms simplify, automate, and stay aligned.

- **Notion or Trello** – Organize business goals, content calendars, family schedules, and even journaling
- **Mint or YNAB (You Need A Budget)** – Budgeting tools that help you track money from a place of *power*, not panic
- **Calm or Insight Timer** – Meditation, sleep stories, and breathwork to regulate emotions in high-stress moments
- **Google Calendar with Time-Blocking** – Color-coded clarity for your wellness, family, and wealth-building zones
- **Canva** – For creating flyers, social media graphics, vision boards, or your next business presentation
- **Audible** – Turn your car rides, cooking sessions, and walks into self-development classrooms

When you automate stress, you free up space for softness, strategy, and success.

Money, Business & Legacy Tools

You don't just make money — you **multiply** it. These tools help you create a financial foundation that honors your lineage.

- **Dave Ramsey Baby Steps** – If you're just getting started, this framework can shift your mindset and momentum
- **QuickBooks or Wave** – Track your business income, invoices, and taxes like a true CEO
- **Ladder or Policygenius** – Get life insurance quotes quickly to protect your children and your generational wealth goals
- **Trust & Will** – Create your will or living trust *now* — not later
- **Acorns or Fidelity** – Micro-investing tools to grow wealth from small, consistent deposits
- **HoneyBook or Dubsado** – Client management platforms for Boss Moms running service-based businesses

Every dollar you align today becomes freedom for your future self — and your children's children.

Daily Practices & Rituals

Small actions = spiritual compound interest. These Boss Mom rituals keep you rooted in your divine identity and mission:

- **Morning Check-In:** Before the world speaks, ask yourself: *How do I feel? What do I need?*
- **Mirror Affirmations:** Speak wealth, power, softness, and clarity into your own eyes every morning
- **Evening Softness Ritual:** Wash the day away — aromatherapy, gratitude journaling, quiet music
- **Weekly Self-Worth Hour:** No chores, no business — just you. Read, nap, create, or *dream*
- **Monthly Legacy Planning:** Review goals, finances, and alignment. Ask: *Is this building the life I want to pass down?*

You don't have to do everything every day. You just have to do what brings you back to you.

Printable Templates & Trackers

Include these in your physical or digital planner:

- **The Boss Mom Daily Planner**
  Morning intention • Top 3 priorities • Affirmation • Mood check • Notes on alignment
- **Monthly Wealth Tracker**
  Income • Expenses • Savings goal • Investment deposits • Financial affirmations

- **Vision Map Template**
  Categories: Health, Family, Spirituality, Money, Career, Creativity, Joy
- **Self-Love Scorecard**
  Track how often you:
    - Rest without guilt
    - Say no with grace
    - Speak lovingly to yourself
    - Ask for help
    - Make space for joy

Words to Speak Over Your Life

The way you speak about yourself becomes the way your life unfolds. Use these Boss Mom declarations daily:

- I am allowed to rest and still be powerful.
- Money flows to me with ease and alignment.
- I do not chase — I attract. I do not beg — I become.
- I protect my peace like it's gold — because it is.
- I am a good mother, even when I prioritize myself.
- I am building a legacy from a healed place.
- My softness is strength. My story is strategy. My voice is valuable.

Speak these over your mirror, in your journal, in your prayers — until your spirit believes them on its own.

Final Reflection

- What tool, ritual, or resource do you need to implement *immediately*?

- What part of your journey are you most proud of — not because it looked good, but because you *grew* through it?
- If your daughter or future granddaughter read this book, what do you hope she learns about who you were?
- How will you protect your softness while building your empire?
- What version of yourself are you finally ready to walk into — no more delays?

Final Affirmation

I am not overwhelmed — I am becoming.
I am not behind — I am in divine rhythm.
I build with clarity. I lead with softness. I mother with wisdom.
Every step I take is sacred. Every choice I make creates legacy.
I am a Boss Mom — and my effect will be *felt* for generations.

Final Blessing: The Boss Mom Sendoff

To the woman who has cried in silence but kept going.
To the woman who has mothered children and dreams at the same time.
To the woman who keeps showing up, even when the world doesn't see her.

I see you.
I celebrate you.
I *am* you.

And I want you to know —
You're not building for applause.
You're building for **alignment**.
For freedom. For healing. For the daughter watching you. For the mother inside of you.

For the woman you're becoming — who's already so proud of you.

May this book be more than pages — may it be your permission slip.
To lead differently.
To build boldly.
To rest deeply.
To love yourself fully.

You are a Boss Mom.

And *this* is your era.

Acknowledgments

This book would not exist without the quiet sacrifices, loud encouragements, and divine whispers that carried me here.

To my three beautiful children — **Eric, Tristian, and Naomi** — you are the heartbeats behind every page. Thank you for loving me through my becoming. Your resilience, humor, and light have given me strength on days I didn't know I had any left. This legacy is for you — and for your children's children.

To my mother, **Becky D. Henderson** — thank you for giving what you had, for showing me endurance, and for helping shape the woman I became. And to my aunt, **Carmelita Green**, your wisdom, laughter, and love have covered me in more ways than I can count.

To my sister, **Tracy Henderson** — your presence, your fire, and your unwavering belief in me have meant more than you'll ever know. You reminded me that sisterhood is not just blood — it's a blessing.

To **God, my Creator** — thank You for the divine assignment. For the strength when I was empty, for the grace when I was uncertain, and for the whisper that said, "Keep going." You are the co-author of my healing, my motherhood, and my abundance.

To my granddad, **James F. Jackson, Sr.** — the first man who showed me what wealth looked like. Not just in finances, but in pride, dignity, and quiet excellence. Your influence planted seeds I am still harvesting today. May you rest in Heavenly peace.

And to every Boss Mom reading this — thank you for letting me speak into your life. May this book be both a mirror and a map. You are powerful. You are enough. And you are never alone.

With love,
Trinetta M. Henderson

---

www.ingramcontent.com/pod-product-compliance
Lightning Source LLC
Chambersburg PA
CBHW021943190326
41519CB00009B/1121